# INDIAN APPAREL INDUSTRY:

## CHALLENGES AND OPPORTUNITIES

By

**Rajendra K. Aneja**

Text copyright © 2020 Rajendra Kumar Aneja

All Rights Reserved.

Dedicated To My Late Parents

Shri Hari Chand Aneja, and

Shrimati Prakash Kumari Aneja

and

My Brother

Narendra K. Aneja.

# THE INSPIRATION

"Seven social sins: politics without principles, wealth without work, pleasure without conscience, knowledge without character, commerce without morality, science without humanity, and worship without sacrifice."

— **Mahatma Gandhi**

## BUSINESS, CONSCIENCE, BROTHERHOOD

"I believe that nothing can be greater than a business, however small it may be, that is governed by conscience; and that nothing can be meaner or more petty than a business, however large, governed without honesty and without brotherhood."

— **Mr. William Lever, The First Viscount Leverhulme**

## COURAGE AND CONFIDENCE

"Show, Courage and Confidence, Not Weakness."

— **Hari Chand Aneja (Daddy)**

# ABOUT THIS BOOK

The Booklet provides an overview and profile of the Apparel Industry in India, impact of various economic and sociological factors on the industry, export-import challenges and opportunities, etc. This Booklet can be a handy guide to professionals in the Apparel Industry and also to consumers.

The Apparel Industry is very challenging and labour-intensive. Manufacturing a garment involves many miniscule processes, to reach it from the factory to the retail shelf. A simple shirt, skirt or jacket, requires multifarious types of materials and accessories, sourced from different parts of the world. These aspects are also touched on.

I thank my colleagues Abhishek Gupta, Gnanesh Mehta, Prachi Pohani, Payal Waghela and Amritaa Aneja, for helping me to organise this Booklet. I am also grateful to Gnanesh Mehta for the pithy cover.

# ABOUT THE AUTHOR

Rajendra Aneja is the Managing Director of a Management Consulting company providing consulting in Sales and Distribution Systems, Rural Marketing, Retailing, Distribution, Business Feasibilities, Productivity, etc.

He worked with Unilever for 28 years in India, Latin America and Africa in a range of General Management, Marketing and Customer Service positions. He has worked in Brazil and later as Managing Director in Tanzania, Africa. He has dealt with a diverse range of products and assignments. Rajendra Aneja has worked in the Middle East, as the CEO of a Retail group and a Foods company.

He was a Sir Dorabji Tata Scholar throughout his graduation from Sydenham College of Commerce and Economics and the Master's Degree in Management Studies from Jamnalal Bajaj Institute. Subsequently he studied at the Harvard Business School and the Harvard Kennedy School of Government.

He has written regularly on rural marketing, economic,

political and sociological topics for a range of journals in India and abroad.

He has authored ten other books viz. "Conquer Rural Marketing Across Countries", "My Experiences in Modern Retail", "Business Express: An Odyssey of Business Ideas, Sensitivities, Engagements & Emerging Global Consumers", "Surviving a Civil War", "Slices & Spices of Life: From Rio to Manila via Dubai, Mumbai, etc.", "A Common Man Writes over One Thousand Letters to the Editor, Volume 1 & 2", "Little Thoughts for a Better World", "Tiny Thoughts for a Bountiful Business" and "Agenda for a New India".

# APPRECIATIONS

"You write very well. Aim to write a book."
>**Mr. Khushwant Singh, Indian Writer and Novelist**

"I hope you will not let this competitive world crush this talent of yours (writing), and will continue to write."
>**Mrs. Jaya Bhaduri Bachchan, Movie Star and Member of Indian Parliament**

"You write very well -- indeed, if you weren't such a senior man with Hindustan Lever, I'd be tempted to ask you if you wanted to join the Digest as a writer!"
>**Mr. Ashok Mahadevan, Editor-In-Chief, Reader's Digest**

"Your excellent article, I read with interest. I was glad you were a recipient of the Sir Dorabji Tata Trust Special Scholarship for six years, which enabled you to train yourself for a career in business management."
>**Mr. J.R.D. Tata, Chairman, Tata Sons Limited**

"I was touched by your article."

**Mrs. Sonia Gandhi, Member of Parliament, President, All India National Congress Party**

"It was nice to read your article which you have written and to know that the work of the Missionaries of Charity is so well established in Chandigarh. I am sure they will benefit from your association."

**Mr. T. Thomas, Chairman, Hindustan Lever Ltd., and Director, Unilever PLC, London (UK)**

"The article that was published in various sections of the media made very good reading."

**Mr. Amitabh Bachchan, Movie Star**

"Human Relations in Retail Management is a crucial aspect which is often neglected. Your work is very relevant to India today."

**Nihal Kaviratne CBE, Former Chairman, Unilever Indonesia. Currently Director Glaxo Pharma, India**

"I knew you were an interesting and talented writer, but I didn't fully realise how prolific. You seem to have a very clear view of today's and tomorrow's worlds."

**Mr. R.D. Morgal, Vice-President, Dale Carnegie & Associates, New York (USA)**

"I have always enjoyed working with you and admired the progress we have made in Tanzania in recent times and wish you all the best in further building the business."

**Dr. Manfred Stach, President Africa, Unilever**

"I want to thank you for your dedication, which clearly went beyond the call of duty, to make Unilever once again a prominent player in the economic growth of Tanzania. All that I did to help in the process was only a facilitator duty: without your personal commitment and that of Unilever, nothing much would have come of it.

I also appreciate your contribution in terms of ideas towards creating a better environment for business in our country, and in terms of wide economic reform and growth through the work of the Tanzania National Business Council.

It would have served us well if you had stayed longer with us, but we wish you equally great success in your new assignment in the Ivory Coast."

**His Excellency, President of The United Republic Of Tanzania, Mr. Benjamin William Mkapa**

"Other multinationals should follow the example of Unilever in Tanzania. The Government recognises your contributions in technology also. You are also promoting capacity utilisation. The government commends and thanks you for that."

**His Excellency, Vice President of Tanzania, Dr. Omar Ali Juma**

"I am very impressed by the efforts and quality of products."

**His Excellency, Prime Minister of Tanzania, Mr. Fredrick Sumaye**

"The growth achieved by Unilever Tanzania, is the envy of any company. About my support when you were building your company in Tanzania. I was glad to be associated with what you were doing, and had great admiration for what you achieved."

### His Excellency, Former British High Commissioner, Tanzania, Mr. Bruce Dinwiddy

"In some countries, simply distributing products to densely populated urban districts and far-flung rural areas represents a major challenge. Tanzania has 100,000 retail outlets across a country with more than 9,000 villages. Half the population lives below the poverty line and earns less than a dollar a day. Our newly established company set up an innovative 'bicycle brigade' of sales people, drawn from local unemployed young people, to supply small shops with products such as Key laundry soap, sold in small units for a few pence. A year after its launch, its affordability and availability earned it an estimated 10% market share."

**Unilever: Social Review**

"I very much hope that the situation in Cote d'Ivoire returns to normal which would give you an opportunity to show your full potential in promoting the growth of your company's operation as you did in Tanzania."

### His Excellency, High Commissioner of India in Tanzania, Mr. Virendra Gupta

"Thanks for your contributions to our business and organisation. You leave Latin America better for having been with us."

**Mr. Charlie Strauss, President, Latin America**

"I read your moving tribute to Tanzania....But what moved me even more was the fact, that the talents of such an outstanding businessman, as yourself are no longer available to a country that needs them so badly."

**Mr. Michael Holman, Africa Editor, Financial Times, London**

"The recent arrival of Unilever has shown that, with the right management, Tanzanians can create top class products."

**Mark Turner, Financial Times, London**

"I enjoyed your nostalgic piece in Indian Express. You have a unique knack of looking at places and people, which is the hallmark of a good raconteur. I expect one of these days you will write a magnum opus."

**Dr. Ashok Ganguly, Chairman, Hindustan Lever Ltd. and Director, Unilever PLC, London (UK)**

"I congratulate you for successfully putting a world class Company on Tanzania's map. It is usually difficult to begin operations in a new country but the manner in which you handled the exercise is commendable."

**Mr. Andy Chande, Chairman Barclays Bank, Tanzania And Tanzania Railways Corporation**

"Your tenure in Tanzania not only established and nurtured your company's business interests so well in Tanzania, but, even more valuable was your approach to the people here – so friendly and full of warm generosity."

**His Excellency, High Commissioner of India to Tanzania, Mr. Dinesh K. Jain**

"Indeed it is your effort, which made Unilever to be what it is today in Tanzania."

**Mr. Melkizedeck E. Sanare, Commissioner General, Tanzania Revenue Authority, Ministry of Finance**

**"'Bicycle brigade' deliver the goods:**

Established only two years ago, Unilever Tanzania's first priority was to create a distribution system to ensure that Unilever products reached its new customers. They did this by using bicycles to distribute Unilever products, in tiny outlets in the villages and slums, naming their new fleet of salesmen the 'Bicycle brigade'. They also used a fleet of vans for the larger outlets in urban areas.

So successful was this pioneering system that in July 2000 Tanzania received the highest award for its 'Distribution and Commercial excellence' from the government of Tanzania. The award was presented to Unilever Tanzania by Sam Nujoma the President of Namibia and William Mkapa the President of Tanzania. It was a state ceremony with a full cabinet present and televised nationally.

The Prime Minister of Tanzania Frederick Sumaye and Iddi Simba the Industry Minister appreciatively said of the new operation:

"It augments availability of good quality products in the villages and slums, generating employment and reducing prices." In light of this achievement, the *Financial Times* reported on the award within an article in a special supplement on Tanzania:

"…..The recent arrival of Unilever…has shown that, with the right management, Tanzanians can create top class products."

*Financial Times supplement on Tanzania, July 24, 2000*

Unilever Tanzania identified that with 100,000 retail outlets across the country, in 25 regions and 9,000 villages that this new distribution system had to be a priority to ensure that the products reached the consumers, even in the most remote and treacherous regions. This shows Unilever's global aim of making daily use products more accessible, available and affordable to consumers and shopkeepers.

Speaking to the Financial Times about the 'Bicycle brigade's mission', Rajendra Aneja, Unilever Tanzania's Managing Director said:

"A systematic distribution operation is crucial to the success of any company in a developing economy. When markets are left to the mercy of the wholesale trade, availability becomes patchy, brands lose their franchise and price indiscipline reigns - this affects sales as consumers do not have freedom of choice." According to Mr. Aneja the system has improved sales fivefold over five months. Omo detergent packs and Blue Band margarine have now become market leaders."

**Global News Unilever Magazine**

# CONTENTS

| Sr. No. | Sections | Page No. |
|---|---|---|
| 1. | **Indian Apparel Industry: Challenges and Opportunities** | 19 |
| I. | Overview of Apparel Industry | 20 |
| II. | Overview of Garment Manufacturing Process | 21 |
| III. | Apparel Market & Segments | 23 |
| IV. | Key Players: Apparel Market | 24 |
| V. | Economic Slowdown & Consumer Sentiment | 25 |
| VI. | Global Turmoil | 27 |
| VII. | Challenges: Apparel Industry | 28 |
| A. | Domestic Market | 28 |
| B. | Export Market | 37 |
| VIII. | Opportunities: Apparel Industry | 42 |
| A. | Domestic Market | 42 |
| B. | Export Market | 54 |
| IX. | Outlook for Next Few Years | 56 |
| X. | Way Forward | 62 |

*Rajendra K. Aneja*

# INDIAN APPAREL INDUSTRY: CHALLENGES AND OPPORTUNITIES

Payal Waghela is a young professional working for a multinational in Mumbai. She is a shopaholic, who loves to shop and keeps herself abreast of the latest fashion trends in the market. This Christmas as she strolled through the High Street fashion outlets like GAP, H&M, Marks and Spencer, Zara and Victoria's Secret, she expected people to be on a shopping spree, buying gifts for their family and friends. However, to her surprise, many retail stores were virtually empty, and in many other outlets only a handful of customers actually purchased clothes.

"Visitors come, touch, feel the garments; then if we are lucky, they may buy a shirt or a skirt," laments Mangesh, a salesman in a retail outlet. Retailers in shopping malls and High Streets, talk softly and in whispers, that their sales are about 10 to 25 per cent lower than the last year. Mangesh regrets, "Naturally my monthly commission is adversely impacted."

Ramakant, a women's apparel retailer, in the unorganised sector, who sits in his 2x2 square metre shop, opposite these High Street fashion outlets, reiterates the decline in consumer demand, saying, "Sales are low, this festive season, compared to last year." However, he consoles, "This could be because of the month-end period. The sales could improve in next month when people get their salaries."

The slowdown in the Indian economy has impacted demand across a range of sectors including food, two-wheelers, automobiles, durables, refrigerators, etc., including readymade apparel. So, this is an opportune time to review the outlook for the apparel industry for the future.

## I) OVERVIEW OF APPAREL INDUSTRY

The Indian textile and apparel industry is one of the oldest and largest in the world, dating back centuries. It accounts for about four per cent of the global market. The industry contributes to about two per cent of the total GDP of India and seven per cent of the industrial output in value terms. It accounts for 15 per cent of the country's total export earnings.

The textile and apparel industry employs about 4.5 crores (45 million) people, making it the second largest employment generating sector in India, after agriculture. Thus, any slowdown in the industry is of importance to the economy. The apparel industry is still largely in the unorganised sector, with small boutiques dominating the sales, particularly in the non-metro cities and towns of India. However, the share of organised sector, which includes domestic and foreign brands, and the private labels of organised retailers, is increasing, due to greater penetration of modern retail outlets, online e-commerce channels and formalisation of the economy.

## II) OVERVIEW OF GARMENT MANUFACTURING PROCESS

To understand the challenges in the apparel industry, it is essential to review the complexity in manufacturing garments. Garment manufacturing is a challenging and labour-intensive industry. A single garment piece such as a shirt or a jacket requires numerous different types of materials. Each material is sourced from different parts of the world, such as Bangladesh, China, Vietnam, etc. The final stock has to be shipped to various markets in India or abroad under tight time schedules.

To manufacture a garment, first the design and the materials have to be finalised, in line with seasons or fashions. Due to concepts of Fast-Fashion and the instantaneous influence of movies and the social media, fashions change rapidly. Then the required materials and accessories such as clothing material, buttons, zippers, threads, laces, elastic, etc., are sourced or imported from various vendors. Each sourcing shipment may have a different delivery time. The production process has to be planned accordingly.

During the production stage, there are various steps involved, such as creating a technical design, matching the material colours with the design, cutting of various parts of the garment, stitching them together as one integrated garment, washing and removal of stains, attaching the price tags and labels, quality checks and audits and finally packing the garment for shipment. Hence, every garment manufacturer has to deal with numerous challenges and compliances on a regular basis. In addition, there are challenges in selling and marketing any garment. Any garment not available in time, can become out-of-fashion. It depreciates in value. This is a challenge that every garment manufacturer and seller manages ceaselessly in this business.

## III) APPAREL MARKET & SEGMENTS

The apparel industry in India has grown at a CAGR of 13 per cent from Rs. 2,432 billion (Rs. 2.43 lakh crores, USD 51.26 Bn.) in 2010 to Rs. 6,484 billion (Rs. 6.48 lakh crores, USD 100.61 Bn.) in 2018. (Exhibit 1.) This is understandable, considering the steadily growing population of the country.

### Exhibit 1 – Indian Apparel Market Size (Rs. Bn.)

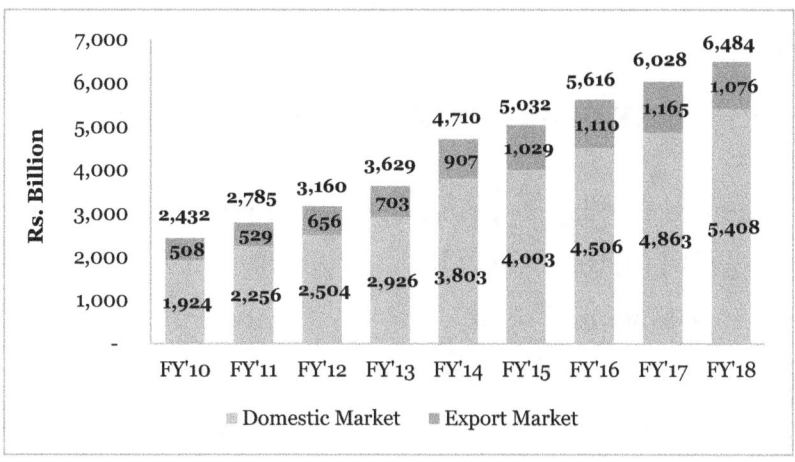

*Source: Credit Analysis and Research Limited (CARE Ratings), Centre for Monitoring Indian Economy (CMIE).*

The domestic apparel (readymade garments) market can broadly be classified into men's wear, women's wear and kids' wear. Men's wear is the largest segment contributing to about 41 per cent of the market. Women's wear and kids' wear account for approximately 38 and 21 per cent respectively of the total market. The Indian apparel market is extremely diverse and varied, due to presence of regional dressing styles, cultural and religious influences and increasing adaptation of western fashion.

The total apparel exports from India in 2018-19 were Rs. 1,128 billion (Rs. 1.13 lakh crores, USD 16.14 Bn.), 4.7 per cent higher than 2017-18.

## IV) KEY PLAYERS: APPAREL MARKET

The pivotal players in the apparel industry in India are Arvind Limited (which has brands like US Polo, Arrow, Flying Machine, Gant, Nautica, Aeropostale, GAP, The Children's Place and Sephora), Madura Fashion and Lifestyle (Louis Philippe, Van Heusen, Allen Solly, Peter England and People), Raymond (Raymond, Park Avenue, ColorPlus, Parx, Ethnix, Manzoni, Zapp and Notting Hill), Siyaram Silk Mills (Siyaram's Suitings and Shirtings, J. Hampstead, Siya, Cadini and Casa Moda), Reliance (Marks and Spencer, Burberry, Armani Exchange, Diesel, Emporio Armani, Gas, Paul Smith,

QuikSilver and Superdry), Garden Silk Mills Limited (Garden and Garden Vareli), etc.

Most of the organisations deliver their garments to the consumers via their own retail outlets, located in malls and the High Streets or through multi-branded garment retailers such as Shopper's Stop, Lifestyle, etc. (shop-in-shop concept). Some manufacturers also sell their brands through online portals like Amazon, Flipkart, Myntra, Shopclues, etc.

## V)   ECONOMIC SLOWDOWN & CONSUMER SENTIMENT

The Indian economy has been in a state of slowdown. The economy grew at 5 per cent in the June 2019 ended quarter, its slowest pace in the past six years. State Bank of India (SBI) estimated the September 2019 ended quarter growth to be 4.2 per cent. In September 2019, the industrial production contracted by 4.3 per cent, the worst performance in last eight years. The automobile industry registered a decline for straight 12 months, with the overall monthly domestic sales falling by 12.8 per cent in October 2019 and the production witnessing a decline of 26.2 per cent.

Unemployment was at a high of 8.5 per cent in October 2019, a three-year high. The rate of unemployment has almost doubled in the past two years. To add to the woes, more than 1,00,000 jobs have been lost in the automobile sector.

The result is that the International Monetary Fund estimated India's economy to grow at the rate of 6.1 per cent (October 2019). The World Bank slashed its projection to 6.0 per cent from 7.5 per cent. The Asian Development Bank reduced the GDP projections from 7.2 to 6.5 per cent and Moody's reduced it from 6.2 to 5.8 per cent. Even the Reserve Bank of India (RBI) lowered its forecast growth from 6.9 to 6.1 per cent, for 2020. SBI sharply cut its growth forecast to 5 per cent from the earlier projection of 6 per cent.

Business Standard newspaper recently reported that the consumer demand in villages has fallen by 8.8 per cent in 2017-18, over 2011-12. Boosting sales despite the slowdown, will be a major challenge in the next few years for the apparel industry.

Mr. Deepak Seth, Group Chairman, Pearl Group of Companies, one of the leading garment manufacturers and exporters, explains that "The 'feel-good' factor is currently missing in the economy, with the general economic slowdown, bankruptcies, etc. Once this 'feel-good' factor returns, conditions will improve."

The slowdown in the Indian economy has also adversely impacted the retail sales of apparel. How to revive the demand will be a major challenge for the businesses in the next few years.

## VI) GLOBAL TURMOIL

The turmoil in the garments industry is global in nature, with the survival of the fittest, as indicated by the Economist Espresso report of 9 January 2020, "The good, the bad and the smugly: Britain's retailers report":

"After the festive season, the reporting season. Britain's supermarkets have been delivering results for the all-important Christmas holiday period this week; today is the turn of Tesco and Marks & Spencer. The story of the past decade is of such venerable behemoths, including the likes of Sainsbury's and Morrisons, missing out to more nimble rivals such as Aldi and Lidl, two German discounters. By the end of the week it should be clear whether this trend continues. The evidence, so far, is that it will. Sainsbury's and Morrisons have both reported drops in like-for-like sales over the holiday period on the previous year. The news from M&S might be bad, especially in clothing. Tesco, however, should do better, continuing its recovery from a nadir in 2015. Aldi, meanwhile, sold 55m mince pies and exceeded £1bn ($1.3bn) in sales for the first time. No signs of indigestion there."

## VII) CHALLENGES: APPAREL INDUSTRY

### A. DOMESTIC MARKET:

#### 1. Battling Rural Distress: Lower Incomes and Spending:

India's growth story was fuelled by agricultural productivity and rising rural incomes. Demonetisation in late 2016 crippled the rural economy which principally runs on cash. These workers live a hand-to-mouth life, subsisting on daily wages. The prolonged agrarian distress, uneven rainfall and stagnant rural incomes have impacted the growth of the rural economy.

Daily necessities like a Lux soap tablet or a Colgate toothpaste tube have acquired the status of luxuries in the villages in many parts of India. In poor rural households, toothpaste has been replaced with "raakh" (ash). A sachet of shampoo has been replaced by black soil to clean the hair. The lunch menu in many such households is just green chillies fried in oil with flattened Indian bread ("rotis"). Such is the economic despondency in the rural hinterland.

Normally, the growth in FMCG products consumption in rural India, outpaces the growth in urban areas by three to four per cent. However, for the September 2019 ended quarter, rural consumption (five per cent) grew at a slower pace than the urban consumption (eight per cent), according to a Nielsen report.

## 2. Rejuvenating the Sliding Demand:

The key challenge confronting the retailers and the apparel industry in India is: How do we prevent a further slide in demand? How do we kindle fresh demand? How do we meet the needs of new customers seeking more value-added garments?

On my visit to a mall in Delhi, Dileep Salecha, a sales manager exclaimed that a customer who used to buy four trousers, now only buys one. Another branded retail store owner, Urvashi Bhaliya was disappointed that her monthly average sale in 2019 has reduced to mere Rs. 20 lakhs (USD 28,600) from Rs. 40 lakhs (USD 62,000) in 2018, i.e. a decline of about 50 per cent.

The average consumer is shy to spend. He wants to hold on to what he has. Even if he has surplus income, he is looking to save, as he is uncertain about the future.

Mr. Rahul Mehta, Ex-President of The Clothing Manufacturers Association of India, says, "Slowdown in the apparel sector is also due to slowing down of sentiments. The overall discretionary spending has gone down. Besides, credit has dried up in the economy, especially for the textile units."

## 3. Consumers: Promotions & Discounts:

Yogita wanted to buy a new shirt. To which, her colleague Manohar opined, "Wait for the Flipkart's Big Billion Day's sale. You could get clothes at a massive discount." Indian consumers are getting habituated to buying with discounts. E-commerce players like Amazon, Flipkart and others offer enticing promotions across categories during festive seasons.

Brand Factory, a chain of multi-brand retail store in India, gives discounts throughout the year. Thus, to be competitive in the market, retailers will have to offer promotions and discounts. Future Group bestows discounts up to 60 per cent on apparels during special sales.

In the next few years, expect margins of retailers to be under pressure and competitive. It will be increasingly difficult to maintain margins with sustained discounting. Fashion retailer, Zara, posted a 13.4 per cent drop in their profits in India for the year ended March, 2019.

The pressure on margins and profitability is not merely an Indian phenomenon. The going is tough on apparel retailers even globally. A renowned international brand, Forever 21, filed for bankruptcy, closing 350 out of its 800 stores, globally. Early this year, US Jeans maker Diesel USA Inc., filed for bankruptcy due to mounting losses and high expenses. Business models will have to be fine-tuned to lower costs sharply in a competitive industry. The cost of every additional button, hook, lapel or sequin will have to be evaluated and a call taken, does the consumer really need it?

## 4. Medium & Small-Scale Enterprises:

The micro, small and medium enterprises (MSMEs) form an important part of the Indian economy. Many of them service the apparel industry. They too need to revive their businesses.

Ashok Mishra, a young retailer selling unbranded garments in Dadar, a crowded but prosperous middle-class market in Mumbai, is forlorn. He is barely able to meet ends through his sales. He says, "The new GST regulations have burdened me with more compliances. I do not even have a laptop!" With the introduction of GST, smaller businesses require technical skills, to comply with the various regulations. This level of expertise is not available with the MSMEs; they are compelled to engage accounting professionals. This hurts their profitability. To exacerbate the woes, the heavy discounts offered by online sites and malls have compelled them to operate on ultra-thin margins.

Moreover, smaller apparel businesses face a liquidity squeeze. Non-banking financial companies (NBFCs) were the main source of finance for the MSMEs. They are not able to source funds easily, especially after the Infrastructure Leasing & Financial Services Limited (IL&FS) crisis. Demonetisation compounded their problems due to cash shortages. The operations of many small garment operators were cash based. A sudden drying up of currency notes crippled their businesses.

With improved flow of currency notes, their problems could ease in the coming years. "A re-introduction of the Rs. 1,000 denomination currency notes would help us smaller retailers," opines Mangesh in Bhuleshwar market. "The Rs. 2,000 denomination notes are too large and the Rs. 500 denomination notes are too small. The Rs. 1,000 denomination notes will help to facilitate transactions. Many a time, I have lost customers for lack of suitable change," he adds.

**5. Changing Trends and Fast-Fashion:**

To survive the downturn and flourish in the future, the apparel industry and the retailers will have to ensure that the latest fashion trends are available in stores at an economical and attractive price. This concept is called "Fast-Fashion".

Fast-Fashion companies like Zara, H&M, Forever 21 and Woolworths, are tantalising consumers with ever changing designs, colours, patterns, trends, etc. The traditional seasons in the fashion industry are disappearing. Fashion has become faster, with flavours of the month, or even weeks.

New Fast-Fashion brands like Uniqlo, a Japanese retail brand, are entering the Indian market. Greater choices and competition from foreign brands will make it more challenging for the domestic players to woo the Indian consumers.

### 6. GST – Flaws & Delays:

In adhering to GST requirements, system issues, delayed reimbursement of input credits, limited knowledge among companies, etc., have frustrated apparel manufacturers and retailers. Delays in GST refunds have choked the cash flows of many businesses. The Government should take the bull by the horns and simplify the GST regulations. All apparel and its inputs should carry a maximum GST of five per cent, to give a fillip to this potential industry.

### 7. Increasing Imports from Bangladesh:

The apparel imports from Bangladesh are increasing in India. As the garments manufactured in Bangladesh are cheaper, these imports pose a strong competition to the Indian domestic manufacturers. In apparels which are not knitted or crocheted, Bangladesh has become the number one import country for India, with Rs. 2,004 crores (USD 286.75 Mn.) of imports in 2018-19. In addition, India imports Rs. 565 crores (USD 80.85 Mn.) of knitted or crocheted apparels from Bangladesh, where it ranks no. 2, followed by China. The imports from Bangladesh in 2018-19 are about 3.5 times the imports in 2014-15. Table 1 shows apparel imports from Bangladesh.

### Table 1: Apparel Imports From Bangladesh, 2014-15 to September 2019 (Rs. lakhs)

| Sr. No. | Garments | 2014-2015 | 2015-2016 | 2016-2017 | 2017-2018 | 2018-2019 | 2019 (Apr-Sep) |
|---|---|---|---|---|---|---|---|
| 1 | Apparel & clothing accessories knitted or crocheted. (HSN 61.) | 18,677 | 23,548 | 21,952 | 31,512 | 56,497 | 35,203 |
| 2 | Apparel and clothing accessories not knitted/ crocheted. (HSN 62.) | 56,414 | 70,871 | 71,896 | 98,045 | 200,380 | 104,311 |
| | Total | 75,091 | 94,419 | 93,848 | 1,29,557 | 2,56,877 | 1,39,514 |

Source: Data for HSN codes 61 and 62, Department of Commerce.

Mr. Rahul Mehta, comments, "There is an increase in imports from Bangladesh. Apparel is imported by brands or retailers in India, say Future Group, Reliance or Arvind, to sell under their own brand names in India. Although the base (value) is currently small, the growth is very evident. It is beginning to impact the domestic sector and is a matter of concern."

## B. EXPORT MARKET:

India manufactures and exports garments to many retailers across the world, including America and Europe. The key apparels exported from India include cotton and other textile T-shirts, men and boy's cotton shirts, baby's knitted cotton garments, women's dresses, blouses or shirts, etc. The top 10 apparels exported from India in 2018-19 are provided below (Table 2).

## Table 2: Top 10 Apparel Export Items From India, 2018-19

| Sr. No. | Apparel Category | 2018-19 (Rs. lakhs) | % Share in Total Apparel | 2019 (Apr-Sep) (Rs. lakhs) | % Share in Total Apparel |
|---|---|---|---|---|---|
| 1 | T-shirts, etc. (Cotton) | 12,90,601 | 11.4 | 6,63,590 | 12.0 |
| 2 | Men's or boys' shirts (Cotton) | 5,70,084 | 5.1 | 2,98,438 | 5.4 |
| 3 | T-shirt, etc. (Other textiles) | 4,85,330 | 4.3 | 2,21,489 | 4.0 |
| 4 | Babies garments, etc. (Cotton) | 4,64,580 | 4.1 | 2,38,470 | 4.3 |
| 5 | Other garments (Man-made fibres) | 4,21,211 | 3.7 | 1,95,548 | 3.5 |
| 6 | Women's or girls' dresses (Synthetic fibres) | 4,16,987 | 3.7 | 2,25,352 | 4.1 |

| Sr. No. | Apparel Category | 2018-19 (Rs. lakhs) | % Share in Total Apparel | 2019 (Apr-Sep) (Rs. lakhs) | % Share in Total Apparel |
|---|---|---|---|---|---|
| 7 | Women's or girls' blouses, shirts, etc. (Man-made fibres) | 3,94,516 | 3.5 | 1,88,491 | 3.4 |
| 8 | Women's or girls' blouses, shirts, etc. (Cotton) | 3,81,913 | 3.4 | 1,55,577 | 2.8 |
| 9 | Women's or girls' dresses (Cotton) | 3,62,769 | 3.2 | 1,79,483 | 3.3 |
| 10 | Men's or boys' trousers, etc. (Cotton) | 3,20,698 | 2.8 | 1,65,881 | 3.0 |
| | Total | 51,08,689 | 45.3 | 25,32,319 | 46.0 |
| | Total All Apparel Exports | 1,12,82,770 | 100.0 | 55,10,559 | 100.0 |

*Source: Export data for HSN codes 61 and 62, Department of Commerce.*

## 8. Higher Costs, Reduced Margins:

Most global retail brands outsource their manufacturing of garments to low cost countries like China, Bangladesh, Vietnam, Indonesia, India, etc. India is a major exporter of garments to top retailers across the world.

However, India has to compete with its cost-effective neighbouring countries like China and Bangladesh, to provide lower production costs, for the apparel business to sustain and flourish. Many raw materials in India cost higher than other Asian countries. This adds to the woes of the Indian manufacturers. Global retailers are increasingly eyeing Bangladesh, Sri Lanka, Indonesia, etc., to source garments. Sourcing materials from abroad, increases the material costs for manufacturers in India.

To compound issues, the apparel industry is highly labour intensive. Wage rates in India are increasing, due to rising costs of living. The cost of capital in India is also high. High-power costs add to overheads. Countries like Bangladesh benefit from lower duty rates in many export markets. So, Indian manufacturers will have to be highly cost competitive to fight global competitors and vendors.

## 9. Trade Barriers, Less Competitive Prices:

Textile and apparel companies in India face higher trade barriers in key markets like the European Union (EU) and USA, as compared to other competing countries like Vietnam, Bangladesh, Pakistan, etc. The average tariff rates on the textile products faced by India, in the EU and USA markets, as compared to others are presented below (Table 3).

### Table 3: EU and USA Tariff Rates (%)

| Sr. No. | Country | EU Tariff Rate (%) | USA Tariff Rate (%) |
|---|---|---|---|
| 1 | India | 5.9 | 6.2 |
| 2 | Bangladesh | - | 3.9 |
| 3 | Vietnam | 6.1 | 5.5 |
| 4 | Pakistan | - | 5.3 |

*Source: ITC Trademap.*

Thus, Indian apparel exporters, face average tariff rates of 5.9 per cent and 6.2 per cent in the EU and USA respectively. Bangladesh and Pakistan enjoy zero per cent tariff in the EU market and a tariff of 3.9 and 5.3 per cent respectively, in the USA. In comparison, Vietnam attracts 6.1 and 5.5 per cent tariff. The high tariff rates, impact the competitiveness of Indian products in the EU and USA markets. In 2018, the exports from Bangladesh increased by 12.7 per cent over 2017. Unfortunately, India's apparel exports declined by 7.6 per cent, during the same period.

## VIII) OPPORTUNITIES: APPAREL INDUSTRY

### A. DOMESTIC MARKET:

**1. Favourable Demographics:**

The Indian apparel market will continue to grow, despite the current economic lull. An increasing young population, higher disposable incomes, migration to large cities, increasing awareness of fashion trends, modern retail formats and apparel branding will boost sales. Indians spent Rs. 5.4

lakh crores (USD 83.91 Bn.) on buying clothes in 2018, a significant jump from the Rs. 1.9 lakh crores (USD 40.56 Bn.) spent in 2010.

The young generation is increasingly becoming fashion conscious. India's youth population (15 – 34 years) is estimated to be 34.5 per cent of the total population of the country, as per Ministry of Statistics and Programme of India (MOSPI).

The urban population has grown from 31.1 per cent in 2011 to 33.2 per cent in 2017. Consumers in urban areas generally have higher income levels and easier access to brands.

Owing to the favourable demographics, the overall apparel consuming market in India, is bound to grow, despite occasional hiccups.

## 2. Growth of Tier 2 and Tier 3 cities/towns:

Nikita visited Vadodara for a vacation, where she owns a small villa. It was during her visit to a local mall, she realised that leading brands like Marks and Spencer, Raymond, Arrow, Peter England,

Calvin Klein, etc., were now easily available in her hometown.

In India, metro cities like Mumbai, Delhi, Kolkata, Bengaluru, etc., are the largest consumers of readymade apparel. For a long time, top fashion brands in the country have focussed on these large cities. However, with the proliferation of e-commerce and the growing mall culture in other towns like Chandigarh, Ludhiana, Kolhapur, Lucknow, Bhubaneswar, Cochin, etc., brands have access to wider markets. For instance, Reliance Group is commencing stores in towns with population as low as 75,000, with rising incomes and aspirations. The increase in the purchasing capacity and the awareness of fashion trends in smaller towns, makes them potential markets.

3. **Value for Money Products:**

Well-known brands like Nike, Adidas, Raymond, Gap, ColorPlus, etc., constantly innovate to lure customers. They sell in own single-brand outlets and in multi-brand stores. They launch new collections every season. To make space for the new inventories, they push the older collections at significant discounts. Middle-class Indians love sales and bargains.

The footfall in the single brand outlets can sometimes be lower than that in the multi-brand stores. Multi-brand outlets have a larger number of promotions to woo customers. Consumers in India are getting habituated to buying apparel at discounts. Rajani, on her visit to a premium apparel outlet noticed that the outlet was almost empty except for a small section, which was crowded. Apparels priced at Rs. 399, cheapest price range for that store, were displayed in that space.

Customers want value for their money. The next few years could be exacting for the economy. Manufacturers of apparel, should focus on popular and low-priced products, to garner market shares.

## 4. Emergence of E-commerce channels:

E-commerce is the future of the retail industry. It has revolutionised shopping models across the world and India. You can get anything and everything delivered at the doorstep, except an elephant or a Boeing aircraft! A consumer can compare various designs and prices, at home for any product. India has the world's second largest internet using population, with 56.6 crores (566 Mn.) users in 2018.

With technology always evolving, e-commerce is set to grow rapidly in the future. The popularity of online shopping in the apparel industry is constrained by consumer's unwillingness to shift from the "touch-and-feel" traditional shopping. However, technologies like virtual dressing rooms, 360 degrees viewing, zoom tools, etc., are being developed to foster online shopping of garments.

Facilities like Cash on Delivery (COD), easy return policy, etc., are convincing the traditional consumers as well to shift to e-commerce. The e-commerce portals provide substantial promotions and a wide range of products, to entice customers. The increasing geographical penetration of the internet and the expansion of e-commerce companies outside the metros, have made a plethora of brands available in the rural and semi-urban areas.

## 5. Reduction in Corporate Tax Rates:

The government has slashed the basic corporate tax rate from 30 per cent to 22 per cent in 2019, in an attempt to revive demand. The rates were reduced from 25 per cent to 15 per cent, for new manufacturing companies.

The reduction in the corporate tax rates may improve the profitability of companies. They may transfer a part of savings to the customers, to incentivise purchases or they may reinvest the additional funds in advertising or promotions. This could boost sales of garment manufacturers in the future.

## 6. Favourable FDI norms:

The government has allowed 100 per cent foreign direct investment (FDI) in single brand retail through the automatic route. Uniqlo, a Japanese fashion brand, will be one of the key brands to enter India under the 100 per cent single brand FDI route. Walmart, which has now acquired the Indian e-commerce business Flipkart, is amazed by the potential for garments in a 1.3 billion people nation. The global premium fashion brand, Kenneth Cole, has also entered the Indian markets with its first flagship retail store in Mumbai.

With new brands poised to launch in India, the market for apparel and fashion could expand in the next few years.

## 7. Sustainable Clothing, "Care for the Environment":

Kushal Shah went in a Decathlon store to buy a new pair of running shoes for a Marathon. While browsing through the store, he spotted a T-shirt which claimed to be made from 100 per cent recycled polyester. The material deployed for manufacturing the T-shirt was made from recycled fabrics (80 per cent) and plastic bottles (20 per cent). Kushal was delighted.

The modern consumer is becoming increasingly concerned about the environment. With growing concerns about climate change and global warming, consumers are getting conscious of what they wear. The established brands like Zara, Levi's, H&M, etc., have also noted this augmented environment consciousness amongst consumers.

Sustainable fashion has led to a drift towards rental clothing, apparel made from recycled material, exchange of old clothes for a discount and other environment-friendly trends, which will find increased acceptance in the future.

## 8. Growth in Designer Wear Segment:

Indian youth is increasingly turning to designer wear on special occasions like marriages, festivals and religious occasions. Indian movie stars like

Priyanka Chopra, Anushka Sharma, etc., and sports celebrities dazzle in Sabyasachi designer wedding lehengas, leaving their fans in awe. Designer Indian wear will continue to blaze in the near future also.

## 9. The Ever-Popular Denim:

Denim garments have been in vogue among the urban masses for many decades. India's rural consumers are also waking up to this rough, steadfast material. Denim has become an essential part of every individual's wardrobe.

Denim can be effortlessly worn in any condition. It is sturdy and durable, making it popular. Denim apparels are low maintenance which makes them more appealing to the consumers, especially in the rural areas. With an increase in the young population of India, the denim market is bound to grow further.

## 10. Prominence of Ethnic & Traditional Wear:

The ethnic wear and Indian fashion segment will continue to flourish. In 2018, it was reported that ethnic wear was the largest category in women's wear segment, with a 71 per cent contribution. W for Women, Aurelia, FabIndia, Biba, Manyavar, AND (Anita Dongre), Soch, Melange, Global Desi, etc., are some prominent Indian ethnic wear brands.

Indian consumers, especially the young in urban areas, have adopted western style apparel, but they also embrace Indian clothing styles. This is demonstrated by the increasing number of ethnic wear brands in the market. In smaller cities and towns, the preference for traditional clothes is very strong. "Kurtis", "salwar-kameez", "lehengas", etc., will continue to reign the wardrobes of Indian consumers.

There is a multiplicity of styles, cultures and traditions in India. Every region has its unique designs, which domestic manufacturers will cater to. The unorganised sector in India will continue to have an edge over foreign entrants. Local suppliers are in a better position to cater to the regional and ethnic tastes of Indian consumers. Local suppliers also sell at more economical prices, as compared to imported brands.

### 11. Growth of Celebrity Brands:

Celebrities and apparel brands have a synergetic relationship. With increasing use of social media platforms like Instagram and Facebook, celebrities are actively followed by their fans. Consequently, many of these celebrities, including the sportsmen and Bollywood artists, have launched their own apparel labels, in the past few years.

Seven (by M.S. Dhoni), Wrogn and One8 (Virat Kohli), True Blue (Sachin Tendulkar), YouWeCan (Yuvraj Singh), Gully (K.L. Rahul), VS (Virender Sehwag), CheQmate (Yuzvendra Chahal), Bhajji (Harbhajan Singh), etc., are some apparel brands launched by cricketers. Being Human (by Salman Khan), HRX (Hrithik Roshan), John Abraham by Wrangler (John Abraham), All About You

(Deepika Padukone), Rheson (Sonam and Rhea Kapoor), Nush (Anushka Sharma), Skult (Shahid Kapoor), Prowl (Tiger Shroff), SSK line (Shilpa Shetty), etc., are some brands launched by Bollywood stars. Many of these brands have even been elongated to other businesses. E.g. Hrithik Roshan's and Tiger Shroff's brands tied up with fitness company CureFit to launch fitness programmes. Katrina Kaif has her own cosmetic products brand, Kay Beauty and Bipasha Basu has her fashion accessory brand, The Trunk Label.

The Indian market will see more new celebrity brands in the future, as social media and mesmerising fan-followings continue to increase.

## 12. Growth of Private Labels:

Organised retail brands are increasingly shifting to private labels across categories. Companies such as Reliance, Future Group, D-mart, etc., are dedicating more space in their stores to their own private labels. The consumers also consider this a worthwhile option, as it provides them additional value for money. They can buy branded quality products, at economic prices. Many retailers have manufacturing and sourcing bases in South Asia, to support the low-cost manufacturing of their private labels.

## B. EXPORT MARKET:

### 13. Diversification: Man-Made Fibres:

More than half the apparels exported from India are made of cotton. Globally, the man-made fibre segment has a much bigger share of the market, compared to cotton. To meet the augmenting global demand for man-made fibres, India should diversify its production to expand the man-made fibre segment in its portfolio.

Mr. Rahul Mehta, says, "We are focussed on very niche segments, e.g. cotton casual wear. We are lagging in the man-made fibre segment, woollen segment, uniforms, winter and sports clothing, etc. These are the areas that we really need to look at, if we want to have a quantum jump, in our exports."

## 14. US-China Trade War:

China is the leading textile and apparel producing and exporting country in the world. The USA is the biggest market for apparel products. The on-going trade tussle between China and the USA will impact the global apparel industry.

The trade tiffs between the USA and China could lead to an increase of tariffs on imported apparels in the USA from the existing 10 per cent. American companies have already started to look at other options to source merchandise. Mr. Deepak Seth, explains, "This trade war between China and USA is creating a huge upheaval in the global supply chain. Many retailers and customers are wary about continuing to work with China. They want to explore other destinations for sourcing. Countries like Vietnam, Indonesia, Bangladesh and India, could benefit by this. This 'China shift' will benefit the good players, who are efficient and operationally strong. Such players are going to benefit by 20 to 25 per cent."

To effectively capitalise and harness the emerging opportunities, India needs a carefully crafted strategy, supporting the growth of apparel exports. Indian exporters need to become lean and mean in costs.

## IX) OUTLOOK FOR NEXT FEW YEARS

**Over-Optimistic Projections:**

The apparel industry is projected to grow between 10 and 26 per cent per annum in the next few years. The industry will have to be creative and innovative to grow at a furious pace. Existing declining trends have to be reversed. The organised and unorganised retail sector in Mumbai city reported a decline in sales in the 2019 festive season, compared to the 2018 season. The textile industry in Surat also witnessed a decline in 2019.

Mr. Rahul Mehta, has hope for a better future, but advocates tighter operating norms, "Performance in the domestic segment is improving. Orders will come but with tight pricing and lower margins. The top line might grow, but maintaining the bottom line will be a challenge."

To revive the industry, the Government has taken up several initiatives like introduction of 100 per cent investment under the automatic route, allocation of funds (Rs. 690 crores, USD 107.06 Mn.) to set up 21 readymade garment manufacturing units, reduction in corporate tax rates, etc. These steps may help the apparel industry to withstand the demand depression and witness growth.

The Government should revive consumer demand, by augmenting the purchasing power of the consumers, generating more employment and increasing public investments, to boost the economy.

**Time to Ignite the Buying Cycle:**

To revive the economy, the RBI reduced key policy rates five times in 2019, from 6.5 to 5.15 per cent. The Finance Ministry has also tried to give a boost to the manufacturing sector by reducing the corporate tax. However, mere reduction in tax rates is not going to fuel consumer demand in the economy.

India has one of the highest corporate tax rates globally. Thus, the move to reduce taxes is wise. Hopefully, the corporate sector will cease the various lay-offs of personnel and the closures of ancillary factories, which were in the pipelines, especially in the automobile sector.

This is also the time to reduce the rate of individual taxation, which at the highest level is over 30 per cent. It is important to kick-start the economy by igniting the buying cycle. It will be smart to put more purchasing power in the hands of the consumers by rationalising the rates of income taxes to a maximum of 20 per cent and lowering the goods and services tax (GST), introduced in 2017, from the highest tier of 28 per cent to a maximum of 15 per cent.

About 45 per cent of the demand for many consumer products comes from India's 6,49,481 villages. The government needs to launch mass employment schemes in rural areas to provide gainful employment to the rural workforce, even when the monsoons and agricultural productivity are erratic. Rural employment opportunities may be found in building roads, in improving agrarian infrastructure with the construction of warehouses, canals, etc., and in animal husbandry, poultry farming and horticulture.

Besides, the Government could also consider following other measures:

1. **Trade Agreements with the EU and USA:** Government should seal trade agreements with important markets like the EU and USA, to give preference to Indian manufacturers.

2. **Reduction in Import Tariff Rates:** Tariff rates on fabric imported for manufacture of export garments, should be reduced.

3. **Assessee Friendly Laws:** An entrepreneur should devote time to grow his business rather than be flummoxed in complying with regulations. Businessmen are entrepreneurs. They generate employment, revenues and provide livelihoods. Laws should be friendly and easy to obey.

**Focus on Customer-Service:**

The apparel industry should focus on the followings:

1. **Understand Consumer Wants:** Young India may prefer cotton and linen garments, or Fast-Fashion at economic prices or durable clothing.

The players should understand the local market and launch suitable offerings.

2. **Emphasis on Customer Service:** Once, I had to return a brand-new unused suit purchased from Marks and Spencer, in UK, after 11 years. To my surprise, they graciously took the suit back, and within minutes fetched full details of my original transaction. Retailers in India should focus on providing excellent customer service before, during and after the sales.

3. **Creative Merchandising and Displays:** Indian retailers should focus on creating attractive product displays, improving presentation of the stores, vibrant interiors, signboards, posters, etc.

4. **Focus on Durability and Quality:** Indians are value and cost conscious. Retailers should focus on increasing the durability of their merchandise.

5. **Training and Development of Staff:** The staffs in many retail stores are ill-informed about

the products, and require training in grooming and etiquette. These issues need focus.

## 6. Suggestions for Small Stores:

The unorganised sector players may also consider the following:

**a) Offer Loyalty Programmes:** Implement loyalty schemes and provide annual rewards, cash-backs and higher discounts, to get repeat customers.

**b) Adapt Computerisation of Accounts:** Computerisation is required for complying with GST norms, easy inventory management, faster billing, etc.

**c) Run Festive Sales:** The unorganised sector could run seasonal promotions and plan communications for their consumers.

## 7. Organised Players: Suggestions:

The organised players may also consider the following:

**a) Save Costs:** Indian companies will have to be highly cost-effective and agile, to remain competitive with international brands.

**b) Focus on Durability and Quality:** Indians are value and cost-conscious consumers. The organised players should focus on increasing the durability of their merchandise.

**c) Expand in Tier 2 & Tier 3 cities/towns:** The incomes and aspirations in the smaller cities and towns will continue to rise in the coming years. The organised players should enter these markets, understand local preferences and launch suitable offerings.

## X) WAY FORWARD

The apparel industry is likely to witness changing trends in the next few years. With the economy under stress, consumers may downgrade and use cheaper brands. Value for money products in the medium to economy price ranges, would be in greater demand.

The retail sector will face augmented pressure from e-commerce stores and malls. They will have to innovate and market aggressively to survive the competition. Nevertheless, expect some brick-and-mortar retailers to shut shop and capitalise on the real estate values of their properties.

Government should reduce its compliances and tax burdens to favour the business community. This is crucial and paramount to revive the economy and ensure growth. The focus should be on an economic agenda to revive growth.

Eco-friendliness is a vital corporate social responsibility. Hence, sustainable clothing trends are set to grow. It is advisable for companies to make their production processes more sustainable in the future.

The next few years may seem daunting and unsure, amidst national and global economic concerns. However, the impact of the slowdown may abate gradually. Value for money products could be the shining stars in the future for the Indian apparel industry.

**By Hari Chand Aneja**

**Available on Amazon**

**By Hari Chand Aneja**

**Available on Amazon**

*Indian Apparel Industry: Challenges and Opportunities*

**Also by Rajendra K. Aneja**

**Available on Amazon**

*Rajendra K. Aneja*

**Also by Rajendra K. Aneja**

**Available on Amazon**

**Also by Rajendra K. Aneja**

**Available on Amazon**

**Also by Rajendra K. Aneja**

**Available on Amazon**

**Also by Rajendra K. Aneja**

**Available on Amazon**

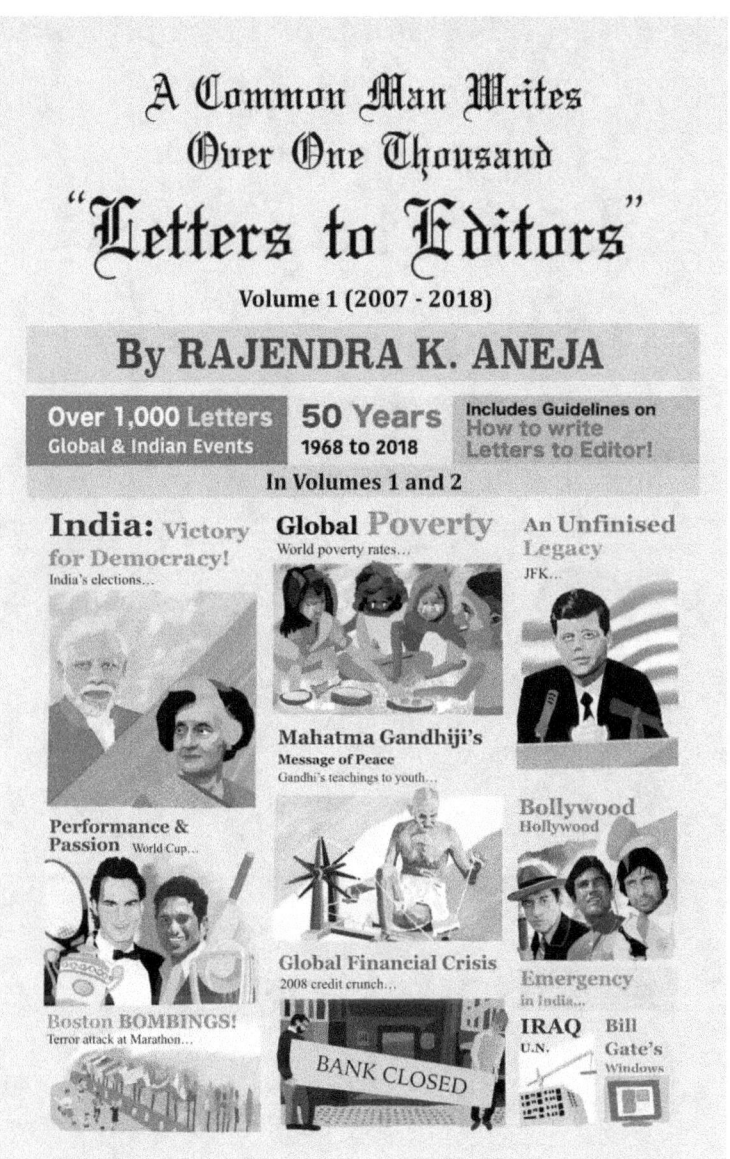

Also by Rajendra K. Aneja

Available on Amazon

Indian Apparel Industry: Challenges and Opportunities

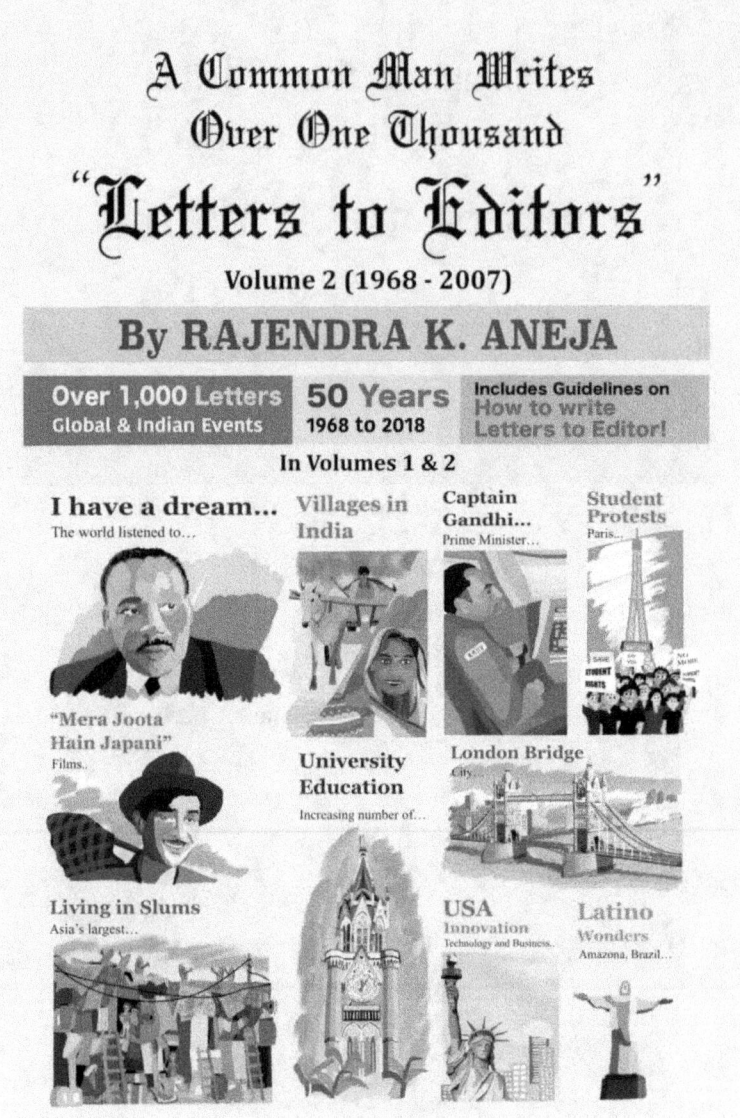

Also by Rajendra K. Aneja

Available on Amazon

**Also by Rajendra K. Aneja**

**Available on Amazon**

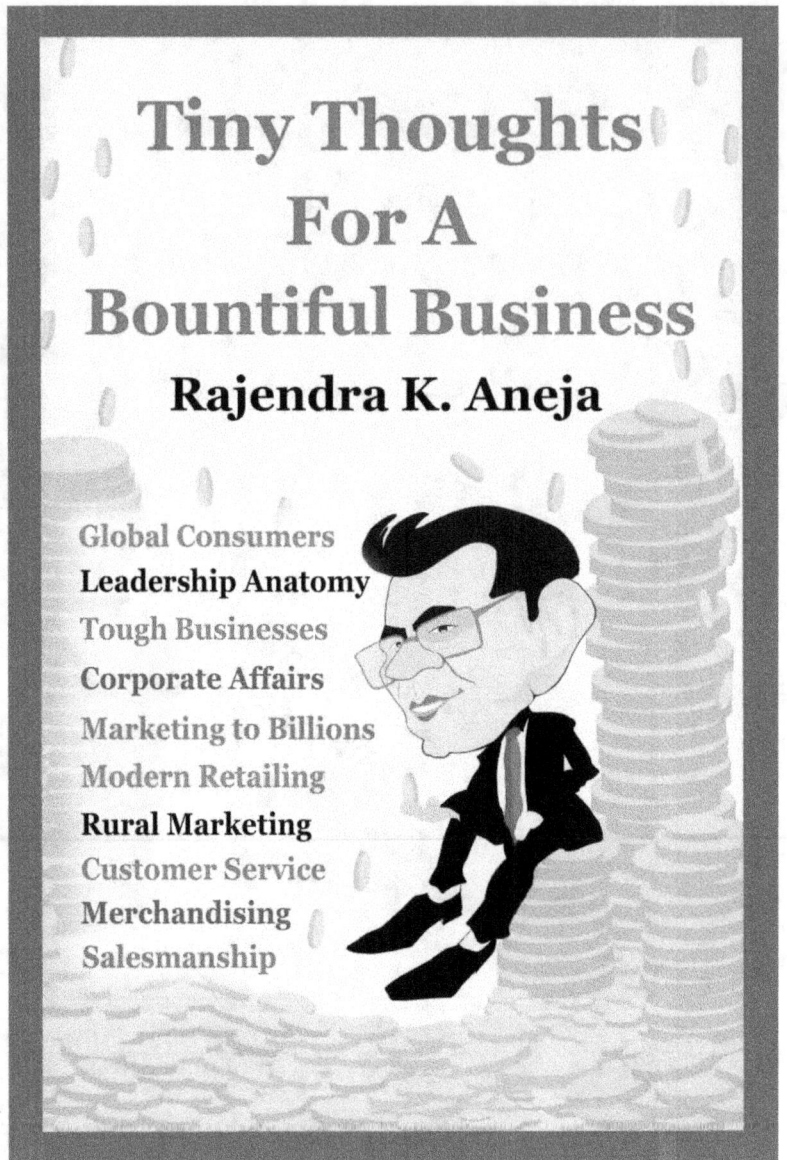

**Also by Rajendra K. Aneja**

**Available on Amazon**

www.ingramcontent.com/pod-product-compliance
Lightning Source LLC
Chambersburg PA
CBHW070816220526
45466CB00002B/682